An Introduction to TCP/IP

John Davidson

An Introduction to TCP/IP

With 30 Illustrations

Springer-Verlag
New York Berlin Heidelberg
London Paris Tokyo

John Davidson
Ungermann-Bass, Inc.
3900 Freedom Circle
Santa Clara, CA 95052-8030
USA

Library of Congress Cataloging-in-Publication Data
Davidson, John, 1946–
  An introduction to TCP/IP.
  Bibliography: p.
  Includes index.
  1. Computer network protocols.   I. Title.
TK5105.5.D379   1988   004.6'2   87–28490

Laser-typeset camera copy provided by the author.
Printed and bound by R.R. Donnelley & Sons, Harrisonburg, Virginia.
Printed in the United States of America.

9 8 7 6 5 4 3 2 1

ISBN 0-387-96651-X Springer-Verlag New York Berlin Heidelberg
ISBN 3-540-96651-X Springer-Verlag Berlin Heidelberg New York

Preface

This book provides an overview of TCP/IP, the *Internet Protocol Suite* developed by the United States *Department of Defense* (DoD) for use in resource sharing computer networks. TCP stands for *Transmission Control Protocol*. IP refers to *Internet Protocol*. The two acronyms together describe not only the protocols, but they also refer to the set of services that collectively allow computer systems (which *host* the services) to connect to one another in order to exchange files, electronic mail and interactive character streams. TCP is in common use in engineering and academic environments as well as within the Federal Government. With the advent of commercial products that supply TCP/IP software (and associated networking hardware), many other businesses can now use this basic set of host-to-host communication services in support of their primary business objectives. This is especially true now that TCP/IP services have been adapted for use in *local area networks* (LANs).

The book groups materials according to the Seven Layers of the ISO Reference Model (discussed in the Introduction), each Layer of which provides a specified level of networking service. The book covers these levels in the following fashion:

- The Physical Level is irrelevant to the protocol suite and is not discussed — though the book assumes the use of TCP/IP on LANs;
- levels two through four are covered each in a separate chapter; and
- levels five through seven are all covered in a single chapter.

Within each group of materials the book covers the following points:

- services identified for that level or those levels by the ISO Reference Model, and
- services specified for that level or those levels by the TCP/IP Protocol Suite.

Acknowledgement

This book was created by members of the software development team responsible for TCP/IP-based local area networking products at *Ungermann-Bass, Inc.* Ungermann-Bass is a pioneering vendor of LAN technology and TCP/IP LAN systems.

An Introduction to TCP/IP was originally written as a tutorial for *Ungermann-Bass* sales and support personnel. The original document was expanded to its present size in order to serve a wider audience when it was perceived that most potential users of TCP products would benefit from an overview of concepts and mechanisms comprising the attendant protocols.

An Introduction to TCP/IP was conceived by Dr. John M. Davidson, Vice President of Software R & D and Chief Technical Officer of *Ungermann-Bass*, who also authored a good deal of the initial manuscript. Additional significant contributors included:

> Stan Mantiply
> Dave Crocker
> George Cohn
> Robert Broberg
> Bart Burstein
> Janet Takami

The author is grateful to Dr. Vinton Cerf, *National Research Initiatives* and to Mr. Dan Lynch of *Advanced Computing Evironments* for review and encouragement in the production of this book.

Mr. Donald Huntington was responsible for preparing the manuscript and producing the final pages using a Macintosh Plus computer with Microsoft's *Word 3.0* and Letraset USA's *ReadySetGo3* page layout program. Ms. Jade Chien provided an excellent review of the text between its original and current form.

Should You Read This Book?

This book does what its name implies — it provides *An Introduction to* the *TCP/IP* Protocol Suite.

The book assumes that you have no familiarity with the TCP/IP Protocol Suite, but that you are familiar with computers in general and with the basic features of LANs, protocols, cabling schemes and networking in particular.

An Introduction to TCP/IP provides some background information on the historical development of the ARPANET and the TCP/IP Community, as well as a description of the role TCP/IP plays in fitting together various pieces of an overall networking scheme.

The main part of *An Introduction to TCP/IP* consists of a description of some of the more important features and protocols that constitute the TCP/IP family. In many cases details are provided concerning the headers, organization and functioning of the parts of the TCP/IP Protocol Suite.

You should be especially interested in this book if you fit in one of the five following categories:

1. MIS Director or Team Member

2. System Engineer

3. Manager of a Government Contracting Company

4. Member of a University or Other Technical-oriented Learning Center

5. Member of an Electronics Company LAN Sales and Service Team

6. Management Team Member Interested in Accessing the Mature Applications Available Through Implementation of TCP/IP

Table of Contents

List of Figures

Introduction

TCP/IP is a collection of network protocols which together support host-to-host communication for hosts connected to any of a number of heterogeneous networks — including land-based, long-haul networks (like X.25 Public Data Networks and the DoD's own ARPANET), satellite networks, mobile packet radio networks and high-speed local area networks such as have recently been standardized by the *Institute of Electrical and Electronics Engineers* (IEEE) Computer Society.

TCP/IP is referred to as an *Internet* Protocol Suite, because it is rich enough to allow hosts connected on different types of networks to communicate with one another (as long as those different networks are somehow *attached* to one another.) The *Department of Defense* (DoD) appropriated the term Internet to refer to the concatenation of *their* many networks into one community, as shown in Figure 1-1. The lower-case term *internet* is used more generally to refer to any collection of linked networks. The distinction is of interest but should cause no real confusion.

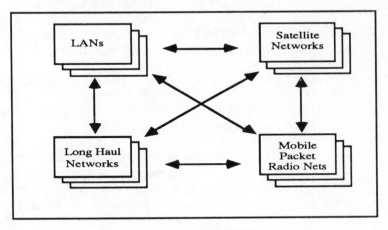

Figure 1-1. The TCP/IP Internet

Origins of the TCP/IP Protocol Suite

In 1969 the DoD built a 4-node, wide-area, store-and-forward packet network, called the ARPANET, as a first experiment demonstrating the feasibility of long-haul packet switching technology. (ARPA is the acronym of the [*Defense*] *Advanced Research Projects Agency* which funded the ARPANET development.) This highly successful experiment was publicly demonstrated in 1972, by which time the net included many university and research sites whose host computers had all implemented a number of protocols used for experimental machine-to-machine (host-to-host) communication. The ARPANET has been used extensively during succeeding years to support computer science and military research projects of many kinds.

The year the ARPANET was demonstrated, work began on a second generation of protocols designed to make use of knowledge gained from the original experiment. By 1982, a *family* (or *suite* or *stack*) of new protocols had been specified, implemented and subjected to extensive experimentation, including four complete cycles or versions. The two premier members of this family are the *Transmission Control Protocol* (TCP) and the *Internet Protocol* (IP). The term TCP/IP now refers to the entire family of protocols.

In 1983, TCP/IP became the standard Protocol Suite used on the DoD Internet, including the ARPANET. During this time a second network, MILNET, was split off the ARPANET, as illustrated in Figure 1-2.

MILNET carries out the tasks of the military research section of the original ARPANET. MILNET and the ARPANET, along with a number of classified networks, are known as the *Defense Data Network* (DDN). *Gateways* exist between the ARPANET and MILNET to facilitate information flow between the two.

The TCP/IP Protocol Suite is probably the most widely implemented, non-vendor-specific protocol of the three currently most popular. The other two are the *Xerox Network*

Systems (XNS) protocols and protocols developed by the *International Standards Organization* (ISO) for *Open System Interconnection* (OSI), the so-called ISO (or OSI!) protocols.

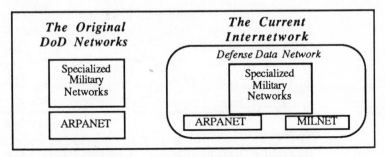

Figure 1-2. Development of the ARPANET

The TCP/IP Community

The ARPA office sponsored the research and development activities of a number of academic and commercial groups, — *SRI International, Stanford University, UCLA, MIT, The Rand Corporation, The University of California at Santa Barbara, The University of Utah, The University of Hawaii, The Institute for Advanced Computation* and *Bolt, Beranek and Newman* (BBN). This *community* of workers invented many of the concepts which permeate today's local and long haul networking technologies.

As noted, TCP/IP is actually the second generation of protocols developed by the ARPA research community. The first generation was the first set of protocols ever created for a variety of independent hosts. That specification employed a host-to-host protocol, the forerunner of TCP, and a host-to-packet-switch (called *Interface Message Processor*, or IMP) protocol which was a forerunner of X.25. The ARPANET, itself a forerunner of Public Data Networks (based on X.25), comprised hosts which connected to a subnet of IMPs. The IMPs provided message delivery for all the connected hosts, just as DCEs in an X.25 network provide message delivery for all their connected hosts. The Host-to-IMP Protocol and the Host-to-Host

Protocol were typically implemented by a program called the *Network Control Program* (NCP) on each host. (The initials NCP sometimes refer as well to the *Network Control Protocol*.)

As important questions were discovered during the creation of the NCP and related protocols, the researchers felt a need to develop a communication mechanism for publishing their thoughts. They began a series of papers, called *Request for Comments* (RFCs), for this purpose and eventually published RFCs which included formal specifications for the resulting protocols.

The TCP/IP project originally circulated papers known as *Internet Experiment Notes* (IENs). After it was decided to migrate from NCP to TCP as the ARPANET standard, only the RFC series was continued. RFCs currently number over 1,000 and now only discuss TCP/IP protocols.

As mentioned, today's X.25 long haul, packet-switching technologies really evolved from work done in the ARPANET, where hosts were directly attached to a subnet whose function is precisely the same as provided by the Telenet or Tymnet subnetworked public packet switching networks today. Six important phases mark development of the TCP/IP Protocol Suite and the utility of TCP/IP-based systems.

1969: The ARPANET

- The ARPANET begins with four nodes at Systems Development Corp., UCSB, UCLA and SRI International. Bolt, Beranek and Newman perform Network management services from their Cambridge, Massachusetts, facility.

- The Host-to-Host Protocol is developed to specify logical connections among hosts connected to the store-and-forward subnetwork. The connection is 'logical' since each thinks itself to be physically connected directly to the other hosts.

1972: The ARPANET Demo

- First International Conference on Computers and Communications provides the initial public demonstration of the ARPANET to prove the feasibility of long-distance packet switching technology. The ARPANET comprises approximately 20 packet switches and 50 host computers.

- The ARPA *Internet Working Group* (INWG) begins exploring issues involved with inter-connecting independent networks.

Mid 1970s: UNIX (DEC PDP-11) and TCP/IP

- *International Federation of Information Processing* (IFIP) Working Group 6.1 complements the work of INWG. This effort leads to TCP.

- UNIX is distributed among academic and research sites.

- TCP undergoing development, research and experimentation.

- Initial TCP implementations made, as prototypes, around the world. The first is undertaken at *Stanford University*, *Bolt, Beranek and Newman*, and the *University College*, London.

- Substantial communication among TCP researchers and *Xerox* (XNS) developers.

Early 1980s: Berkeley UNIX

- PDP-11s are giving way to VAXs. Berkeley provides 4.1 BSD and 4.2 BSD UNIX for these systems, containing NCP and TCP implementations.

- Continued movement towards use of TCP/IP as official military standard.

1983: TCP/IP Replaces NCP

- ARPANET converts from NCP to fulltime TCP.

- The ARPANET splits into two pieces — one retains the original name, the other is called *MILNET*. Both networks employ the same subnetwork hardware, routing and packet switches (BBN C-30 IMPs).

- TCP/IP published as Military Standard specifications.

- Sun Microsystems brings TCP/IP into widespread commercial environments. The technical world adopts TCP/IP quickly, though business tends to wait for ISO's completion.

1995(?): ISO Replaces TCP/IP

- It will take a while for the ISO Protocol Suite to replace TCP/IP.

- ISO specifications are still evolving and implementations lack the broad range of services found in TCP/IP, particularly with respect to the interaction of interconnected networks.

- The strengths and deficiencies of TCP/IP are well understood and many people know how to build products to the protocol. ISO implementers will spend a number of years before reaching that same degree of experience.

The OSI Reference Model

The services of the TCP/IP Protocol Suite can be identified
and arranged according to a careful taxonomy or scheme as
outlined by the *International Standards Organization* (ISO)
seven-level *Open Systems Interconnection* (OSI) Reference
Model, as shown in Figure 1-3.

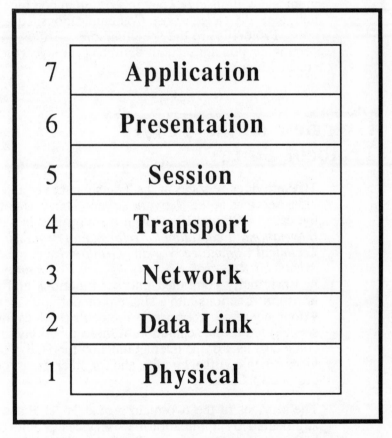

Figure 1-3. Levels of the OSI Reference Model

The OSI Reference Model describes the functions provided by any networking system in terms of layers — where each layer builds upon lower ones. The Reference Model is actually *a communications service specification*; each layer provides a particular kind of service to the layer above it and expects a particular kind of service from the layer below.

To provide communication services, each layer must communicate with its *peer layer* in a different communications unit, typically called a host. Communications require protocols. Protocols are the specifications or rules governing communication transactions between peer layers of the Reference Model.

Overview of the TCP/IP Protocol Suite

TCP provides services at the Transport Layer and IP provides services at the Network Layer. This was not always the case. TCP and IP evolved from proposals within the *International Federation for Information Processing* (IFIP) *Technical Committee Working Group 6.1* and the *Defense Advanced Research Projects Agency Community*, which had originally combined internet functions and reliable transport functions into a single protocol. Subsequent development of other Transport Protocols (such as for packet speech) led to the separation of these functions so that IP could take care of the internet function for TCP, which provides reliable virtual circuits, and for other Transport Layer protocols as well.

The services of the two main protocols, TCP and IP, are augmented by application-like services provided in the higher layers. As mentioned, the term TCP/IP refers to a large family of protocols and services. Some of the protocols are displayed in Figure 1-4. There are a variety of implementations of all of these.

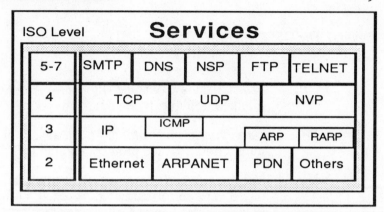

Figure 1-4. Some TCP/IP Protocols and Services

The Figure shows that IP and the higher-level protocols may be implemented on several kinds of physical nets. The ARPANET, Ethernet and the X.25 Public Data Networks are pictured individually, while MILNET, IEEE 802.3 CSMA/CD, IEEE 802.4 Token Bus, and IEEE 802.5 Token Ring nets are collectively referred to as 'Others.'

The protocols' names are acronyms for terms indicating their function. Below is a list of some core services the protocols provide. (The list, of course, includes the TCP and IP protocols themselves — which loaned their names to the entire protocol suite.)

Level Three — *Network Layer*

IP: *Internet Protocol* — Provides internet transaction services for Layer Four clients. Generally thought of as providing Host-to-Host datagram delivery.

ICMP: *Internet Control Message Protocol* — Used by Gateways and hosts in the Internet to apprise other hosts of conditions related to their IP services.

ARP: *Address Resolution Protocol* — Maps an IP Address into an associated Ethernet Address.

RARP: *Reverse ARP* — Maps an Ethernet Address to an associated IP address.

Level Four — *Transport Layer*

TCP: *Transmission Control Protocol* — A connection-oriented, reliable, byte-stream protocol.

UDP: *User Datagram Protocol* — An unacknowledged transaction-oriented protocol parallel to TCP.

NVP: *Network Voice Protocol* — Real-time transaction-based service for carrying digitized, compressed voice.

Levels Five through Seven — *Session, Presentation* and *Application Layers*

SMTP: *Simple Mail Transfer Protocol* — Provides for sending text mail between hosts — a major function of the military/government/research networks.

DNS: *Domain Name Service* — Provides directory services. DNS is a complex, distributed Internet service for mapping a name to an address.

NSP: *Name Service Protocol* (IEN #116) — An early, simple service for mapping host names to IP Addresses.

FTP: *File Transfer Protocol* — Permits exchange of complete files between computers.

TELNET: *Telecommunications Network* — Provides virtual terminal services for interactive access by terminal servers to hosts.

All of the TCP/IP protocols have been implemented numerous times — some for experimental purposes, some for commercial. Users with widely varying computer equipment may choose from among a number of hardware and software components from several networking vendors and *roll their own* integrated system. As an example, consider a typical Ethernet system as depicted in Figure 1-5 below.

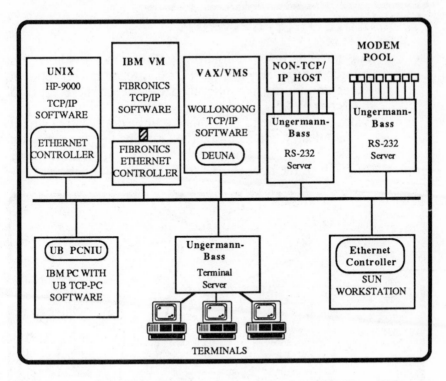

Figure 1-5. Network Products Accessible with TCP/IP on Ethernet

A Sample Internetwork

As stated earlier, the goal of TCP/IP is to provide for the intercommunication of hosts, PCs, terminal servers and other computing paraphernalia on one or more types of LANs or WANs (*Wide Area Networks*). Figure 1-6 provides an example of how this could be done with a simple system design connecting three facilities in two cities within the U.S. This figure motivates the discussions of the remainder of the book.

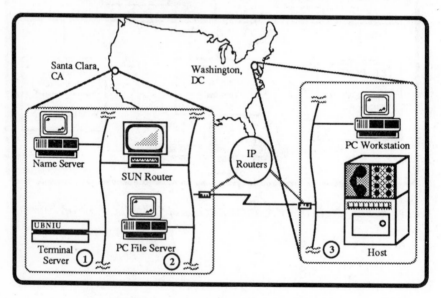

Figure 1-6. A Sample Internetwork

The concepts are quite simple. The above figure shows three LANs — two in Santa Clara, CA and one in Washington, DC. Packets of data can flow among hosts on any of the three Local Area Networks, and can flow from a host on one network to a host on another, as long as the networks are somehow *attached*.

Figure 1-6 shows that networks 1 and 2 are *attached* by a SUN Workstation, and networks 2 and 3 are attached by a long distance telecommunications link and a pair of boxes called *IP Routers*.

In each case, the task of the devices providing attachment is to route packets from one LAN to the other. Packets between hosts on networks 1 and 3 will have to go through both the SUN and the paired IP Routers in order to reach their destination. Packet routing is the responsibility of the Network (IP) Layer of protocols in both the hosts and the routers. Reliable communication, on the other hand, is solely the responsibility of the Transport (TCP) Layer of protocols in the hosts.

As an example of what might be done on such a nationwide internet, consider that a user at in interactive terminal in Santa Clara might wish to access the computing services of a host in Washington. In that case the user instructs the terminal server to open a TCP connection through the internet to the host. The terminal server and the host then exchange TELNET characters on the connection in order to effect the desired service.

Additionally, consider a PC user in Washington wishing to access data stored on the PC File Server in Santa Clara. In that case the user instructs the operating system to treat one component of file storage as a remote component. (Of course, the operating system must be prepared to do this. Several PC systems have been extended to allow such *redirection* — for example, Microsoft's MS-NET and IBM's PC-LAN.) The operating system will then call upon its networking code (on PCs this code is usually called NetBios and is available for many network types using many different protocol suites — for example, Ungermann-Bass's version of TCP/IP) to open a TCP connection to the File Server in Santa Clara. The two PCs will exchange a private protocol (called the *Shared Message Block*, or SMB, protocol) on their TCP connection in order to achieve the desired file sharing.

The Name Server is another interesting component in Figure 1-6. The presence of a Name Server underscores the difficulty of finding hosts and file servers in a network or internet. If you know the name of a target resource, then a name server may be able to provide its internet (IP) address so you can send it a packet. Of course, the Name Server must somehow itself acquire the name and address data; and the source system must know how to extract such data from the Name Server.

Obviously, a user wishing to integrate terminals, PCs and hosts into a meaningful internet must consider the need for a Name Server. This book does not discuss techniques for doing all these. Early mechanisms were described in IEN #116. Newer mechanisms are being provided by *Domain Name Service* protocols, which are discussed in a series of RFCs.

Level Two
The Data Link Layer

The lowest level of the ISO Reference Model that is important to our discussion is the Data Link Layer, as shown in Figure 2-1.

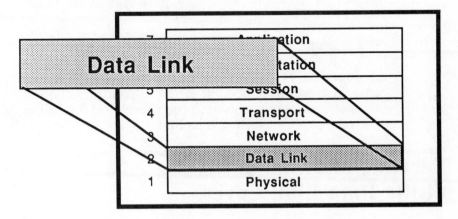

Figure 2-1. The Data Link Layer

The *Data Link Layer* in LANs supporting TCP/IP provides for passing discrete pieces of information, called *frames*, between participating stations that are directly connected to the given LAN. Peer Data Links in LAN systems provide relatively modest services, aside from frame delivery. Data transmitted at this level undergoes little processing, though generally it is protected by hardware checksums to aid in error detection.

Data Link services in WANs, such as the private wide-area ARPANET or public wide-area X.25 networks, are more comprehensive than those in LANs. Hosts in these kinds of nets are attached by point-to-point links to a packet-switching node which, in conjunction with other such nodes, provides store-and-forward processing for IP packets through the net, ultimately delivering each in a frame passed to the target host. Since these wide-area nets often attempt to provide reliable packet delivery, it is necessary for the Data Link services of the host to provide reliable frame delivery to the packet switch on the assumption that the switch cannot reliably deliver a packet which it does not reliably receive.

LANs and WANs have differing Data Link characteristics which IP at the Network Level hides from higher-level protocol modules. Therefore, it should be possible to discuss the TCP/IP technology without providing information about Level Two.

As a convenience, however, this chapter will discuss the Data Link services of Ethernet LANs. Ethernet has become the dominant TCP/IP networking technology. But, because TCP was developed prior to the standardization of Ethernet, special protocols have been developed for the use of IP on top of the Ethernet Data Link.

Services and Standards at the Data Link Layer

Local Area Networks divide the Data Link Layer into two sub-layers, as shown in Figure 2-2.

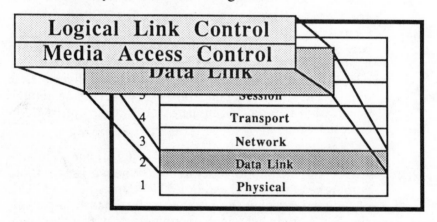

Figure 2-2. Dividing the Data Link Layer

The lower, *Media Access Control* (MAC) sub-layer, dictates how the medium is to be shared by the multiple stations. The upper one, the *Logical Link Control* (LLC) sub-layer, provides the types of services normally associated with the more conventional *Data Link Control* (DLC) mechanisms in point-to-point systems, such as addressing, checksumming, etc.

The Logical Link Control services extend typical DLC point-to-point services by ensuring that multiple, logical links can be multiplexed into a single network station as though it had many separate physical point-to-point links to remote peers.

In 1981 Digital Equipment Corp. (DEC), Intel and Xerox created the Ethernet *de facto* standard for local area networking. The IEEE 'cleaned up' the Ethernet specification, making it more to its liking, legitimating it as a standard specification, and giving it the catchy title, *802.3*.

The original Ethernet and the later 802.3 both employ a *Carrier Sense Multiple Access with Collision Detection* (CSMA/CD) transmission technique which permits stations to contend for use of the transmission medium without the necessity of globally-coordinated access management .

An important standard which doesn't use CSMA/CD is the IEEE's 802.5 *Token Ring*. The Token Ring circulates a token past the 'front door' of all the stations in the ring. The token is like a permission slip to communicate. When no one is communicating, the token circulates around the system unused. Before transmitting, a station on the network waits for the token to come by and modifies it so it becomes unavailable to others. Then the station transmits its message. When the message comes all the way back around the ring, the station changes the token back into a free one and removes its own message. The token then continues its path around the ring, unused until another transaction begins.

A third standard, the IEEE's 802.4 *Token Bus*, uses a linear topology to accomplish the same thing as the Token Ring — that is, stations are physically on a shared bus (like the Ethernet) but are sequentially organized so they operate as though on a ring. The Token Bus creates a circular pat-

tern of token rotation among a set of linearly organized stations. It accomplishes the difficult task of making the linearly organized stations operate like the circular arrangement
in the Token Ring by explicitly sending the permission slip
from one station to another. The MAC protocols of the
Token Bus are particularly intriguing when stations attempt
to enter or leave the logical ring.

Ethernet

The TCP/IP community is working on techniques for providing TCP/IP services on each of the IEEE standard types
of Data Links. Techniques for providing TCP/IP on Ethernet have already been determined. Ethernet packets use
Data Link frames, as shown in Figure 2-3.

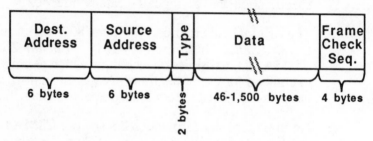

Figure 2-3. Ethernet Frame

Ethernet frames have Destination and Source Addresses
which are 48 bits in length. They also carry a 16-bit Type
field that identifies the format of the packetized information
found in the variable length Data field. The Data Link
Layer uses the Type field to separate received packets destined for one network layer (e.g. IP) from those destined
for another (e.g. XNS's *Internet Datagram Protocol*).

All IP transactions carry the value X'0800' as their *Ethernet Type* (in contrast to X'0600', the XNS transaction
type).

A variation of standard encoding for IP packets over an Ethernet involves *Berkeley-style trailer encapsulation* (described in RFC #893). Trailer encapsulation is the technique of placing IP headers behind rather than ahead of higher level protocol information in an Ethernet Data field. Trailer encapsulation was designed to reduce processing time by hosts in certain, limited circumstances. The Berkeley style packet is illustrated in Figure 2-4.

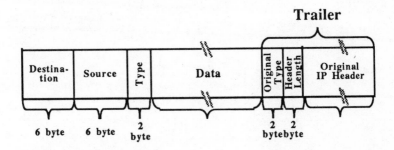

Figure 2-4. Berkeley-Style Trailer Encapsulated Packet

Trailer encapsulated frames come in three sizes, containing higher level protocol information in one, two or three 512 byte blocks. The Ethernet Type field is equal to X'1001', X'1002', or X'1003' to distinguish the three sizes and to identify this unique packet format.

Level Three
The Network Layer

For most networking tasks, the minimum underlying 'raw' data transfer service provided by the Data Link Layer is, by itself, too limited. Much more power for transmission of data on networks and between networks is provided by the *Internet Protocol* (IP) at the Network Layer — ISO Level Three. As part of its end-to-end packet delivery function, IP provides many additional transmission services. For example, it provides enriched addressing in order to permit identifying stations by both Network Number and host Node Number. It also provides Fragmentation and Reassembly in order to surmount any limitation placed by the Data Link upon the size of a frame, thereby permitting large IP datagrams to transit networks that have a small maximum packet size.

It is possible, using Network Layer services, to create internetworks of independent LANs and to send packets from a node on one LAN to a node on another. The forwarding of packets requires routers (sometimes called gateways) which are nodes attached to two or more networks. They forward a datagram based upon its destination IP address. Remote router-linked networks are physically distant from each other and use a pair of routers to connect two networks over a telecommunications link, to make the two nets operate as one. Local routers directly connect two networks, without a telecommunications link.

Four important protocols available at the Network Layer, including IP, ICMP, ARP and RARP, as illustrated in Figure 3-1. The hexadecimal values for the associated Ethernet Type field are also shown.

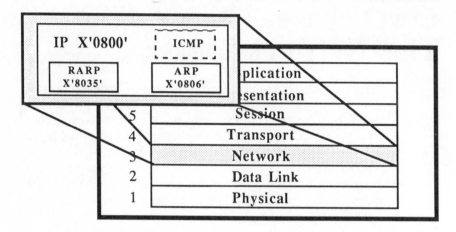

Figure 3-1. Protocols in the Network Layer

Internet Protocol (IP)

Within the DoD Internet Protocol Suite, the principal protocol of Level Three is IP. Its job is to interconnect one or
more packet-handling networks into an internet. It provides
its services to various *Upper Layer Protocols* (ULPs) by
assisting the delivery of ULP data through the internet in
one or more IP datagrams. (This is the service that the *Internet Datagram Protocol* — IDP — performs for XNS.)

The internet architecture permits a two-level hierarchy of
logically-independent networks. The top level is a flat collection of *peer* networks. A network is allowed to com-
prise a flat collection of *peer sub*networks. Networks and
subnetworks may contain directly-attached hosts, as illustrated in Figure 3.2.

The distinction between networks and subnetworks only
involves the way that IP addresses are interpreted and depends upon the location of the IP module specified by the
address. For most discussions, *subnetworks* can be called
networks. This document uses the word 'subnetwork' only
when it is important to distinguish the internet hierarchy.

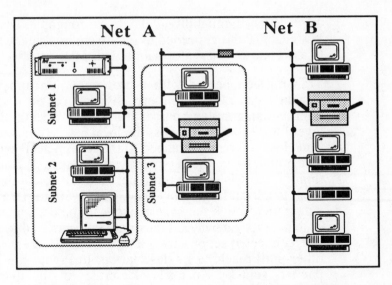

Figure 3-2. Logical View of IP Internet Structure

IP Overview ·

IP is limited to the basic functions required for delivering a
datagram (*block of data*) through an internet. Each IP datagram traversing an internet is an independent entity, unrelated to any other datagram. The host's IP Layer provides
services *to* Transport Layer protocols and relies on services
from the Data Link layer. The IP layer takes data sent by a
Source Transport entity and uses the services of its Data
Link Layer to forward the data to the IP Layer of the destination host. IP does not promise a reliable service. Hosts
receiving IP datagrams will discard datagrams when insufficient resources are available for processing and will not
detect datagrams lost or discarded by the Data Link layer.

IP insulates upper layer protocols from network-specific
characteristics. For example, IP maps internet addresses
supplied by ULPs into Data Link Addresses appropriate for
the immediately attached network. Also, IP accommodates
any packet-size restrictions of intermediate networks along
the transmission path within the internet.

Additional services that IP provides include selectable levels of transmission behavior involving such characteristics

The Network Level

as precedence, reliability, delay and throughput. IP also allows data labeling, needed in secure environments in order to associate security information with data.

Transmission begins with a protocol in an upper layer passing data to IP for delivery. IP packages the data as an internet datagram and passes it to the Data Link protocol layer for transmission across the local net. When a destination Host is directly attached to the local net, IP sends the datagram through the net directly to the Host. When a destination Host is on a remote network, IP sends the datagram to a local IP gateway. The gateway, in turn, sends the datagram through the next network to the destination host or to another gateway. A datagram thus moves through the interconnected set of networks from one IP module to another until reaching its destination. In Figure 3-3 below, packets sent by Host #1 take either of the two paths shown.

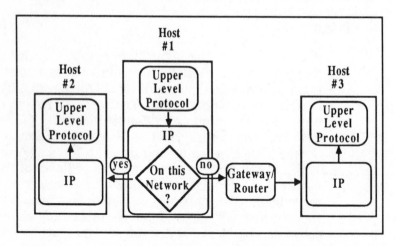

Figure 3-3. Transmission via IP

Gateways, also called *IP Routers* (and sometimes 'Local Bridges' or 'Remote Bridges') are datagram relays interconnecting two or more networks or subnets. Each gateway contains an IP module residing above two or more Data Link protocol entities.

The sequence of IP modules handling the datagram in transit is called the *Gateway Route*. A gateway route is distinct from the lower level, node-to-node route supplied by a particular network or subnetwork. In other words, a network may itself consist of a set of packet switching nodes which connect hosts on the network to one another. Long haul networks typically contain such switching units. LANs, such as Ethernet, typically do not. The gateway route is based on the network/subnetwork field of the destination internet address.

IP modules share common rules for interpreting internet addresses in performing internet routing. Gateways make routing decisions on an individual datagram basis.

A gateway attached to two or more networks must decide which network should be used *next* for any datagram which it handles; it must also decide whether the ultimate destination host is on the *next* network (in which case the datagram can be sent directly to that host) or whether an intervening gateway should get the datagram in order to relay it on to a distant net. To determine which gateway should be the next to handle any datagram which requires further relaying, a given gateway must know its options. It must somehow acquire information about other gateways and about the paths available to it to reach any specified destination net. It is best if this reachability information can be acquired and maintained dynamically according to the instantaneous connectivity provided by all the gateways of the internet. To accomplish this, gateways need to exchange reachability information with one another. Over the years a number of gateway-to-gateway protocols have been developed which seek to provide for this information exchange.

Gateways which connect a set of privately owned and managed networks can use any protocol they desire. In general, any such private protocol is termed an *Interior Gateway Protocol* (IGP). In IP parlance, each independently administered internet is called an *Autonomous System*.

Gateways which cross administrations (in particular, say, gateways which lead from private facilities into the DDN) must employ what is called the *Exterior Gateway Protocol* (EGP). EGP is a simple, well-defined and official protocol described in RFC # 904.

The Network Level

IP Header

Function and field allocations in the IP Header are illustrated in Figure 3-4 and defined in the accompanying text.

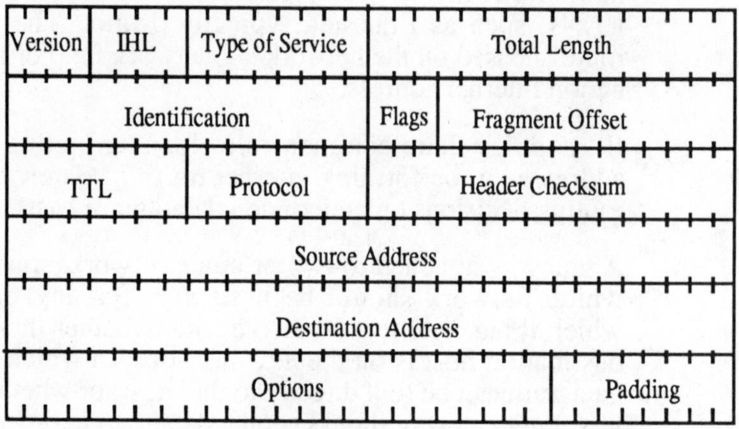

Version	IHL	Type of Service	Total Length		
Identification			Flags	Fragment Offset	
TTL		Protocol	Header Checksum		
Source Address					
Destination Address					
Options				Padding	

Figure 3-4. IP Header

Subsequent sections present more detailed descriptions of important concepts.

Version Abbrev: VER

Field size = 4 bits

- The Version field indicates the format of the IP header. The book describes Version four — current at the time of writing. Versions 1-3 are now unused.

- The Version field declares the version of the protocol to which the datagram belongs. Including the version in each datagram provides the possibility of developing new protocols while the network is in operation.

Internet Header Length   Abbrev: IHL

> *Field size* = 4 bits
> *Units* = 4 Octet Group
> *Range* = 5 - 15 (default=5)

- Internet Header Length is the length of the IP Header, expressed in 32-bit units.

- The Internet Header Length field is required since the IP Header contains a variable-length Options field.

Type of Service   Abbrev: TOS

> *Field size* = 8 bits

- The Type of Service field contains the IP parameters describing the quality of service desired for this datagram.

- The field permits the host to specify to transit networks the kind of service desired. The field allows specification of datagram precedence, desired reliability and expected resource consumption, as discussed later in the text.

- Type of Service is specified in order to inform the transit networks of the service desired. The networks may or may not be able (or willing) to accommodate the stated desires.

Total Length   Abbrev: TL

> *Field size* = 16 bits

- Total Length is the length of the datagram, measured in octets, including IP header and data portions of the datagram.

Identification   Abbrev: ID

> *Field size* =   16 bits

- An identifying value used to associate fragments of a datagram. The sending ULP usually supplies this value as an interface parameter. If not, IP generates datagram identifications which are unique for each sending ULP.

- The Identification Field supplies the datagram number to permit the destination host to determine to which datagram a newly arrived fragment belongs, as the text will later describe.

Flags

> *Field size* =   3 bits

- This field contains the control flags *Don't Fragment* (which prohibits IP fragmentation) and *More Fragments* (which helps identify a fragment's position in the original datagram).

- The Don't Fragment flag is supplied for use with hosts that may lack the ability to put fragmented datagram pieces back together. Many implementations of TCP/IP, in fact, do not support fragmentation and reassembly.

Fragment Offset Abbrev: FO

> *Field size* =   13 bits
>   *Units* =   8 Octet Group
>   *Range* =   0 - 8191, default=0

- This field indicates the position of the fragment's data relative to the beginning of the data carried in the original datagram. Both a complete datagram and a first fragment have this field set to zero.

- Fragment Offset locates the current fragment's position in a datagram as a multiple of eight bytes (the elementary fragment unit). Thirteen bits are provided. Therefore, a maximum of 8,192 fragments are permitted per datagram. This will, in turn, permit a maximum datagram length of 65,536 bytes (consistent with the Total Length field).

Time-to-Live   Abbrev: TTL

> *Field size* = 8 bits
>   *Units* = Seconds
>   *Range* = 0 - 255 (255=4.25 minutes)

- This field indicates the maximum time the datagram may remain in the internet. When the value drops to zero, the datagram should be destroyed.

- The unit of time in measuring Time-to-Live is seconds, so a maximum lifetime of a datagram is 255 sec. (rather than 256 seconds — since a zero value destroys the datagram).

- The value is decremented by at least one for each router through which it passes.

Protocol   Abbrev: PROT

> *Field size* = 16 bits

- This field indicates which ULP is to receive the data portion of the datagram. The numbers assigned to common ULPs are available from the DoD Executive Agent for Protocols. Some are listed in Appendix Two — 'Assigned Numbers.'

- The Protocol field specifies the particular Level Four protocol to which the datagram belongs (e.g., TCP, or some other equivalent).

Header Checksum

Field size = 16 bits

- Contains the checksum covering only the IP Header.

- Checksum aids in the detection of certain errors. The algorithm is simply to add up the one's complement of each data item (as 16-bit words) and then to take the 1's complement of the sum.

- The Checksum in the IP Header verifies the condition only of the IP Header. When passing through a gateway, the Header changes (e.g., the TTL Field is decremented by one) and the Checksum is recomputed.

Source Address Abbrev: SOURCE

Field size = 32 bits

- Contains the Internet Address of the datagram's originating host.

Destination Address Abbrev: DEST

Field size = 32 bits

- Contains the Internet Address of the datagram's target host.

- The Source and Destination Addresses indicate the network number by using eight to 24 bits. Bits not used for network identification are used to refer to the host number and, optionally, the sub-network number, as the book will later discuss.

Options   Abbrev: OPT

>   *Field size*   = variable

*   Provides an escape to permit later versions of the proto-
    col to include information not present in the original de-
    sign, to permit experimenters to try out new ideas and to
    avoid allocating permanent header bits to rarely-needed
    information.

*   The length of this field depends upon the number and
    types of options associated with the datagram.

The officially-defined *options* specify:
*   *Security* — Labels Level, Compartment, User Group
    and Handling Restriction, as required by the DoD.
*   *Loose Source Routing* — Permits the sender to require
    the datagram to follow a general internetwork path.
*   *Strict Source Routing* — Requires a specific path.
*   *Record Route* — Traces the path taken.
*   *Stream ID* — Permits a gateway to handle collections of
    datagrams in a similar way. Stream ID is similar to a tai-
    lored virtual circuit service.
*   *Timestamp* — Permits a time-trace of a datagram's route
    through the internet.

Fragmentation and Reassembly

Networks always impose a maximum size on packets because of:

- hardware limitations (e.g., width of a transmission slot)
- software limitations of a particular operating system (e.g., buffers are 512 bytes),
- protocols being used (bit restriction in packet length field),
- restrictions imposed by a standard,
- error-reduction measures, or
- time limitation on packets in a channel.

The list in Figure 3-5 demonstrates the variety of maximum packet lengths imposed by various network schemes:

Network Name	Maximum (in bits)
Bell Labs' Spider	256
University of Hawaii ALOHANET	640
X.25 (default)	1,024
ARPA Packet Radio Network	2,024
The ARPANET	8,192
X.25 (maximum)	8,192
Ethernet	12,144

Figure 3-5. Maximum Packet Length by Network

Level Three IP Datagrams in transit may traverse a subnetwork whose maximum packet size is smaller than the size of the datagram. To handle this, IP provides fragmentation and reassembly mechanisms. When a gateway is faced with sending a datagram into a network which cannot accommodate it as a single packet, it must fragment the original datagram into pieces, called *datagram fragments*, that are small enough for transmission.

IP datagrams may be routed independently so that fragmented datagrams may not meet until they reach the destination host and may even arrive out-of-order. Hence, all receiving hosts are required to support reassembly.

The IP module in the destination host will reassemble fragmented datagrams into a single datagram for delivery to its Transport Client. Figure 3-6 illustrates the process of fragmentation. (For clarity the illustration is simplified and doesn't include complete headers, etc.)

Note that not all protocol suites deal with fragmentation and reassembly in the same way. XNS, for example, requires reassembly to be done by the network that did the fragmentation, which simplifies the implementation for receiving hosts. XNS imposes a significant restriction on internetwork routing and upon the characteristics of the 'final' (receiving) network, since the sending and receiving networks must accommodate packets of the same maximum size.

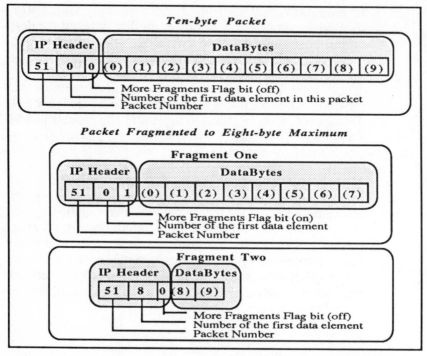

Figure 3-6. Fragmentation of 10-byte Packet on 8-byte Maximum Packet Size Network

Setting Parameters

IP can tailor its services to support a diverse set of *Upper Layer Protocols* (ULPs). A transport protocol with real-time requirements, such as the *Network Voice Protocol* (NVP) can use IP's datagram service in a way that differs from the method used by TCP, for example.

This section describes the ways in which ULPs can identify the services that will be offered by IP and tailor those services in a particular networking configuration.

IP's Tailorable Services

IP's delivery service can be customized to suit the special needs of an Upper Layer Protocol. For example, if it is desired to have a given datagram traverse a particular gateway route on its way to a destination, such a predefined route, called a *source route*, can be supplied by the ULP. Each IP module knows to forward the datagram according to the specified source route — perhaps augmented, if necessary, by the standard routing mechanism.

Tailorable IP network parameters fall into two categories: *service quality parameters* and *service options*. Service quality parameters influence the transmission service provided by intervening gateways; service options are used to invoke special processing within IP modules. These are both discussed below.

Service Quality Parameters

ULPs which know that their datagrams will be going through intervening gateways may suggest to the gateways that certain kinds of treatment be given to each of their packets. These suggestions are made in the Type of Service parameter.

Precedence — Instructs the gateway to attempt preferential treatment for high-importance datagrams. Preferential treatment might prevent such datagrams from being delayed in a queue within the gateway, for instance.

Transmission Mode — *Datagram* vs. *stream.* Datagram mode (the default) indicates that the ULP considers this datagram to be a sporadic event, unrelated to past or future datagrams. Stream mode asks the gateway to minimize delay and delay dispersion for a flurry of similar datagrams through reservation of network resources.

Reliability — Attempts to minimize data loss and error rate. A parameter ensuring that as queue resources are depleted datagrams requesting low reliability are discarded in favor of those requesting high reliability.

Resource Tradeoff — Designates whether it is more imporant to honor the request for high precedence or high reliability in case the gateway cannot supply both.

The notion of *stream mode* vs. *datagram* is not often used in local or long haul networks but is used by broadcast satellite networks, since satellite routers can often request transmission bandwidth on their shared channel in advance. If they detect that packets are beginning to arrive with the *stream mode* bit set, they can anticipate the arrival of more of those packets and thus request from their peer stations larger amounts of future bandwidth to ensure that an arriving datagram will not be delayed while making bandwidth requests in real time. (Satellite routers cannot talk to one another instaneously; their packets have a minimum one-quarter second transmission delay.)

Service Options

The IP Header may be expanded to include several optional fields which provide IP services in source, destination and intermediate (routing) nodes. Examples of defined options include:

Security Labeling — Identifies the security level (secret, top secret, etc.) of the datagram for classified hosts.

Source Routing — Selects the set of gateway IP modules to transit, according to specifications by the sender. Permits a node to choose the networks through which a given packet must travel or to designate networks through which it must not travel, thus enhancing the security or privacy of certain types of transactions. Source Routing may be specified as 'loose' (the gateway may take some liberties) or 'strict.'

Route Recording — Records transited gateway IP modules so the destination host can see where a datagram has been.

Stream Identification — Identifies the stream to which a given datagram belongs; used with the stream service.

Timestamping — Allows gateways to mark the moment at which they processed the datagram.

Don't Fragment — Marks a datagram as an indivisible unit which should not be fragmented by the gateway.

Error Reporting Service

Certain errors detected by Data Link protocols or reported by peer IP modules must be indicated by a host's IP Layer to the interested Upper Layer Protocol. These indications depict several classes of errors, including invalid arguments, insufficient resources and transmission problems. Errors that IP will report to ULPs are usually determined for each IP implementation.

Matching IP Addresses to Network Configurations

One of IP's goals is to provide services in a great variety of networking and internetworking environments. IP's addressing mechanism has thus been designed to allow for three different classes of possible network configurations. The three IP Address classes, labeled A, B, C, provide for internetworks which have:

- A — many hosts on few networks;
- B — a medium distribution of hosts and networks; and
- C — few hosts on many networks

This is illustrated by Figure 3-7.

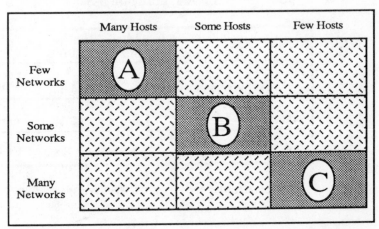

Figure 3-7. Types of Networks

Only 32 bits are available for expressing a complete IP Address, which consists of both a network designation and a host designation. An internet with only a few networks will require only a few bits for the network designation. By convention, these will be the high order bits of the 32 bits available for addressing. On the other hand, an internet with many networks will require more bits for the network designation — and thus will eat further into the 32 bits on the high order side.

Within a network, hosts may be arranged into smaller communities, called subnetworks. The layout of IP Addresses allows for the designation of subnets within the 32 bits of the IP Address by masking off certain bits to be used as subnet identifiers. The concept of subnets and subnet masks is described in RFC #950, which discusses subnetwork routing. The mask provides a structure for the bits of the host designation. For example, a campus may have a Class B address, which requires two bytes for the Network portion and two bytes for the host portion. Rather than have 65536 host addresses, it might choose to divide the campus into 254 subnets (one byte) with 254 hosts per subnet (the other byte). (Only 254 subnets and hosts are possible, since the values '0' and '255' are reserved.)

The IP addresses, masks and formats for the three classifications are as follows, in Figure 3-8.

Class	Initial Binary Bits	Number Net Bits	Number Host Bits	32-Bit Hex Net Mask
A	0XX	7	24	FF000000
B	10X	14	16	FFFF0000
C	110	21	8	FFFFFF00

Figure 3-8. Classifying Network Types

Upon presentation of the 32-bit number, how is it determined whether this is a Class A, B or C address? The way to tell is from inspection of the first bits. If the first (the high, or most significant) bit is zero, then the address is Class A. If the first bit is one, it is necessary to examine the second bit; if that bit is zero, the address is Class B. If the second bit is one, on the other hand, it is necessary to look at the third bit. Right now the third bit is always zero so the address is always Class C. A value of one for this bit designates a Class D, which is not currently in use.

All the possible combinations are shown in Figure 3.9

Class A	1st bit 0		
Class B	1st bit 1	2nd bit 0	
Class C	1st bit 1	2nd bit 1	3rd bit 0
Class D	1st bit 1	2nd bit 1	3rd bit 1

Figure 3-9. Possible Network Types

An IP Address is often displayed as four fields separated by a dot, each field being one byte (valued 0-255). The difference in interpretation of these fields depends upon which of the four possible classes the IP represents. Note how the 4-byte notation permits identification of a network's class by examination of the value of the first byte.

Value	*Class*
0-127	A
128-191	B
192-223	C
224-255	D

Figure 3-10. Designating Network Classes

Designations of the three classes are made according to the values illustrated in Figure 3-10.

Note that a Class A Address might be 10.1.17.1, a Class B address might be 128.203.5.17, and a Class C might be 192.1.2.10.

Services IP Requires from Lower Layers

IP not only provides services to ULPs; it requires support from the lower levels, including *transparent data transfer between hosts within a single subnetwork* as well as *error reporting*. Datagrams may not necessarily arrive in the same order they were supplied to the subnetwork layer, nor is data guaranteed to arrive free of errors. The lower layers provide reports to IP indicating errors from the subnetwork and lower layers, as feasible. The specific error requirements of the subnetwork layer are dependent on the individual subnetworks. Ethernet, unlike the long haul networks, does not generally report errors except, for example, when a particular packet needs to be discarded because of 16 consecutive collisions. Since IP datagram delivery is not considered infallible, how an IP module will react to information from a lower layer about the disposition of a particular packet is largely unspecified.

Internetwork Control Message Protocol (ICMP)

Packet recipients use ICMP to tell sending IP modules that some aspect of the sender's behavior should be modified. ICMP is usually generated by a station which perceives an error or problem in a packet that somebody else has sent. This may be perceived either by the destination host or by an intermediate gateway. A gateway or destination IP module will occasionally encounter an error or problem during datagram processing. These events may be reported via ICMP. If a packet is undeliverable, ICMP may be used to alert the packet's source that the network, machine or port is unreachable. ICMP also can inform the sender of preferred routes or of network congestion. Further, a simple datagram-echoing service is defined.

ICMP is officially part of IP. However, ICMP datagrams are sent *using* IP. That is, it is a functional part of Layer Three but is encoded as if it were a Layer Four Protocol.

Address Resolution Protocol (ARP)

All stations and gateways are represented by an IP Address — which is limited to 32 bits. Sending things over an Ethernet requires at least 48 bits just to identify the subsequent 'hop' (next gateway or ultimate destination node) in the *Ethernet's Destination Address* Field (DA). How is it possible to get 48 bits out of 32? Obviously it's impossible. One can't merely 'invent' additional bits. Furthermore, Ethernet addresses are arbitrary: no two stations have related addresses. Therefore, another set of services must be provided at the Network Layer on an Ethernet which can request a mapping from a 32-bit IP value into a 48-bit Ethernet address to be used for the next hop of the packet. ARP was invented to do this.

When a source Network Layer is presented with a packet whose Internet Address is specified but whose Ethernet Address is not, that Network Layer may broadcast an ARP request in order to learn from a more knowledgeable source on the network what the next hop Ethernet Value should be. Someone must respond to the ARP request — usually the Destination IP station itself. When a response is received, the 48-bit address can be maintained in a cache so the next time a request is presented for that same IP Address, the Ethernet Address can be retrieved from the cache and the ARP protocol transaction can be avoided.

The host resolves destination addresses in the following way: It looks for a cached Ethernet DA. If not there, it calls ARP to broadcast an address request. As an alternative, the host may also use addresses contained in a configuration file. Note the three typical sources for DA values when sending a datagram:

1. responses to the ARP broadcast requests;
2. the cache of addresses from earlier ARP responses; and
3. configured information.

The Network Level

The service specification for ARP permits it to convert an IP datagram into the ARP request. Since this consumes the datagram, the ULP must be prepared to reissue that datagram, if appropriate. Since IP functions in an unreliable environment, this usually looks to the Transport Layer as a packet that has been lost.

Internet Address Resolution

ARP locates hosts that are on the sender's own network or subnetwork. It's utility is limited by the reach of an Ethernet broadcast. To send to a host on another network, the datagram is first directed to an IP router attached to the sender's network. In this case, the sending host must determine the Ethernet address of the router which, in turn, will forward the datagram to its recipient.

Proxy ARP

Some IP Routers respond to an ARP request on behalf of a distant recipient. The sender is fooled into thinking that the remote recipient is responding. Hence, this is called *Proxy ARP*. Its use is not generally recommended, but is required when a sending host's IP is not sophisticated enough to determine that the packet must be sent to the Router.

Reverse Address Resolution Protocol (RARP)

Suppose the only thing a station knows at initialization is its own Ethernet Address, usually from configuration information supplied by its manufacturer. It could obviously learn its IP Address from preconfigured data. On the other hand, it could attempt to learn this information at initialization time. The RARP protocol serves this purpose. RARP allows a station to send out a broadcast request in the form of a packet that asks, "Who am I?" That is to say, "What is my IP Address?" Obviously, somebody (typically a RARP Server) must be prepared to do the inverse of ARP — taking the 48 bit Ethernet Address and mapping it into an IP

Network and Node number. This only happens at startup. RARP is not run again until the next time the device is reset or turned off and restarted.

A value of X'8035' in the *Ethernet Type* field indicates that the packet is a RARP Packet. (Note that there must be a RARP server on each Ethernet segment, since broadcasting is used, and broadcasts are not forwarded by IP Routers.)

IP on IEEE 802 Networks

IEEE 802 frame formats differ from the format used for Ethernet. In particular, IEEE 802.3 networks do not have an Ethernet Type field; that field is used to specify the frame length. Additional fields specify the *Link Service Access Point* (LSAP) and the *Subnetwork Access Point* (SNAP) information, as defined by IEEE 802.2. These protocols are not yet officially adopted for use by IP but appear likely to gain acceptance.

SNAP will provide a standardized method of encapsulating IP datagrams on the three 802 network cable schemes. It also will provide a standard for implementing IP-related protocols, such as ARP. The encapsulation will be performed as indicated in Figure 3-11.

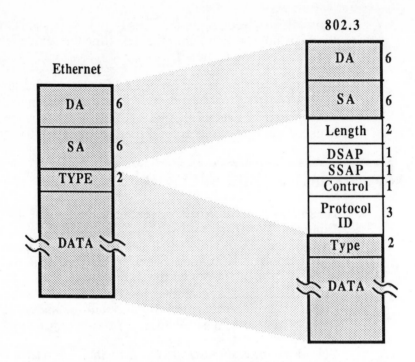

Figure 3-11. Position of the SNAP Header

The *Destination* and *Source Service Access Points* (DSAP
& SSAP) are expected to be X'AA' to indicate the presence
of a SNAP header; one SNAP Protocol ID will be assigned
(possibly the value zero) to indicate that an encapsulated
Ethernet frame follows. The Ethernet Type value will indicate whether or not the frame is in IP format.

Level Four — The Transport Layer

The Transport Layer is level four of the OSI Reference Model (see Figure 4-1).

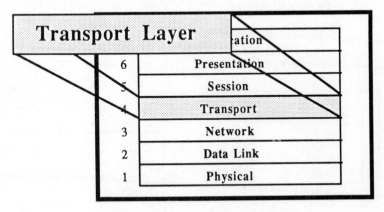

Figure 4-1. The Transport Layer

Services Identified for the Transport Layer

The Transport Layer is designed to provide a machine with end-to-end subnet-independent connection and transaction services. The lower layers of the ISO Model are concerned with the transmission, framing and routing of packets between machines. The Transport Layer, however, has the task of providing reliable and efficient end-to-end transmission services between processes rather than simply between machines. All four levels work together to provide a complete transport service — providing robust and transparent communication upon which the upper levels of protocols may then build.

The Transport Layer is where the popular concept of *virtual circuits* is effected. Virtual circuits are implemented by associating a series of packets with one another. The goal of this associating is to provide a service by which applications can talk with one another just as though they had a physical point-to-point link. A Transport protocol accomplishes this service by splitting an application's data into a sequence of packets and then managing the transmission (and retransmission) of these packets so as to provide delivery of data in order, without duplication or omission.

TCP/IP provides two principal protocols at Layer Four — the *Transmission Control Protocol* (TCP) and the *User Datagram Protocol* (UDP), as illustrated by Figure 4-2.

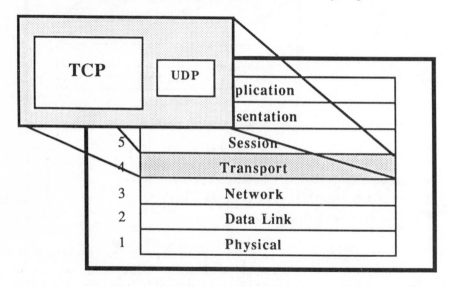

Figure 4-2. TCP & UDP at the Transport Layer

Other Transport protocols have been specified, such as those used for the transmission of digitized voice, but these are beyond the scope of this book.

Transmission Control Protocol (TCP)

TCP is designed to operate over a wide variety of networks and to provide virtual circuit service with orderly, reliable transmission of user data. TCP serves as the basis for a reliable inter-process communication mechanism on top of unreliable subnetworking of packets where loss, damage, duplication, delay or misordering of packets can occur. It is a complex protocol — having to deal, for example, with detection of lost packets, automatic retransmission and pathological problems like the handling of delayed duplicate packets.

The potential for providing robustness in the face of unreliable media makes TCP well-suited to a wide variety of multi-machine communications applications. TCP supports interconnected networks. It was specifically designed to operate above IP, which is at ISO Layer Three (the *Network Layer*), as illustrated in Figure 4-3.

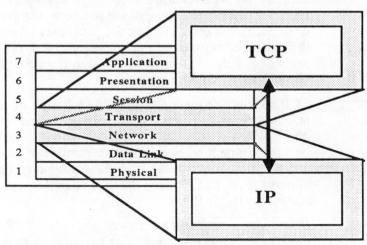

Figure 4-3. TCP & IP Relationship

TCP Overview

TCP has the task of providing reliable communication between pairs of processes in logically-distinct hosts on networks and sets of interconnected networks. It provides connection-oriented transfer at the Transport Layer — the same basic service as the XNS *Sequenced Packet Protocol (SPP)*.

TCP supports a wide range of *Upper Level Protocols* (ULPs) which need to send data to their peers on other hosts. TCP does not attempt to impose any structure on the data sent by a given ULP. It treats ULP data as though it were a continuous *stream*, thereby leaving all notions of message structure in the hands of the ULPs themselves. (This is contrasted with XNS's SPP which helps provide message boundary demarcation for its clients.) TCP does, however, attempt to segment the stream into discrete units so it can be sent and received in individual packets. Each such unit is called a *segment*.

Because TCP is designed to be independent of particular network characteristics, it has a generalized definition of the concept of packets (or segments) that allows them to be as long as 65K bytes. Peer TCPs may send segments to one another that are any size up to that maximum. If they actually try to exchange such large segments, most IP Layers will have to fragment the segment into many lower level packets in order to meet the packet size constraints of their attached network. In practice, most TCP implementations deal with segments whose size is *just right* for the network to which they are attached.

TCP assigns a sequence number to each *octet* of its client's *infinite* stream. (An octet is just 'a byte dressed up in a tuxedo.') When it exchanges segments with its peer, TCP labels the segment with the sequence number of its first octet and the number of octets which the segment contains. This allows the peer TCP to put the data back into a continuous stream for its ULP.

If forced to retransmit a series of segments, TCP is free to repackage the data — combining two small segments into a larger one, for example. This mechanism, motivated by a desire for line efficiency in long haul networks (where the number of header bits relative to data bits is of concern), makes TCP more complex than other Transport protocols, since a receiver has to deal with segments that contain some octets it may have previously seen and some which are new.

The Transport Level

Figure 4-4 illustrates the entire transmission process from an originating ULP through TCP to a destination TCP. The process is discussed in the following text.

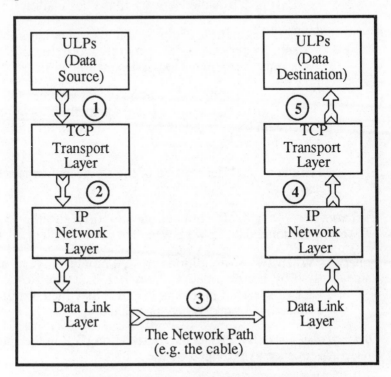

Figure 4-4. The Transmission Process

The numbers in the diagram refer to the following steps in the data transmission process:

1. Source *Upper Level Protocols* (ULPs) send a data stream to TCP for transmission.

2. TCP breaks the stream into segments, possibly providing for full-duplex exchanges with *timed retransmissions, ordering, labeling of security and precedence levels, flow control*, and *error checking*. It then passes the segments to the IP.

3. IP performs its services on the segments (creating data-grams, carrying out fragmentation, etc.) and transmits the datagrams through the Data Link and Physical Layers across the Network to the destination IP.

4. The destination IP does whatever checking and reas-sembly processes are required and delivers the data-grams as segments to the destination TCP.

5. The destination TCP carries out its services (as in #2), restoring the segmented data to their original data stream form and delivering the data stream to the desti-nation ULPs.

Here is a fuller description of the services mentioned in #2 above:

Full-duplex — A TCP connection supports simultaneous bi-directional data flow between the correspondent ULPs.

Timely — When system conditions prevent timely delivery, as spec-ified by a user timeout parameter, TCP notifies the local ULP of service failure and the ULP may then terminate the connection, or take other special action.

Ordered — TCP delivers data to a destination ULP in the same byte sequence as provided by the source ULP.

Labeled — TCP associates with each connection the security and precedence levels supplied by the ULPs during connection establishment. When information is not provided by the ULP pair, TCP assumes default levels. TCP establishes a connection between a ULP pair only when security/ compartment information supplied by the pair exactly matches. Each TCP segment is labeled with the negotiated security value. If a security mismatch occurs during the connection, TCP will terminate the connection.

Flow controlled — TCP regulates the flow of data across the con-nection to prevent, among other things, internal TCP con-gestion, leading to service degradation and failure.

Error checked — TCP delivers data that is free of errors within the probabilities supported by the checksum.

The Transport Level

TCP Header Format

The TCP Header is a relatively enormous creature. The header, together with a minimum-size datagram (and the associated IP Header), is 40 or more bytes (not bits!) in length. Functions and memory allocation in the TCP Header are illustrated in Figure 4.5 and explained below.

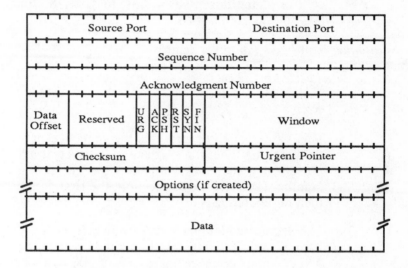

Figure 4-5. The TCP Header

Source Port   Abbrev: SRC PORT

Field size = 16 bits

This is basically an address which identifies a process or service in the Sender's host. The Source Port does not form a part of the IP Address; however, the combination of the IP Address and Port Number uniquely identify what is called a *socket* or point of access into a given process.

Destination Port   Abbrev: DEST PORT

> *Field size* = 16 bits

- This is an address which identifies a process or service in the Receiver's host.

- The *Source* and *Destination Port* Fields are under the control of the hosts. Each host may decide for itself how to allocate its ports.

Sequence Number   Abbrev: SEQ

> *Field size* = 32 bits
> *Units* = Octets
> *Range* = 0 - 2**32 - 1

- This value usually represents the sequence number of the first data byte of a segment. However, if a SYN is present, the sequence number is the Initial Sequence Number (ISN) of the connection; the first data octet is then numbered ISN+1.

- The Sequence Number and Acknowledgment Fields are both 32-bits in length, thus allowing for specification of a very large sequence space. (At 1,000 bytes per second, one could send for nearly 50 days before wrapping the number. Given that maximum packet lifetimes are expressed in terms of seconds, its is not likely that packets with old sequence numbers will be delivered so late that their sequence number will have come up again causing them to look as if they were current.)

Acknowledgement Number   Abbrev: ACK

> *Field size* = 32 bits
> *Units* = Octets
> *Range* = 0 - 2**32-1

- If the ACK control bit is set, this field contains the value of the next sequence number that the Sender expects to receive.

Data Offset

> *Field size* = 4 bits
>   *Units* = 32 bits
>   *Range* = 5 - 15, default = 5

- This field indicates the number of 32-bit words in the TCP header. From this value, the beginning of the data can be computed. This information is needed since the Options field is of variable length. The TCP header (even one including options) is an integral number of 32 bits long.

Reserved

Field size = 6 bits

- Reserved for future use. Must be set to zero.

Control Flags

Field size = 6 bits

- The *Control Flags* field carries a number of single-bit indicators which are used to establish, terminate and maintain connections.

- *URG* Urgent Pointer field significant. URG=1 indicates that the Urgent Pointer field is being used to locate urgent data, by means of a byte offset from the current sequence number. This serves the function of an interrupt. If the flag is not set, the Urgent Pointer field is to be ignored.

- *SYN* Used to establish connections; SYN=1 is a connection request.

- *ACK* Acknowledgment field significant. ACK=1 indicates that the Acknowledgment field is relevant.

- *RST* Can reset a connection in the event of delayed duplicate SYNs, host crashes and other reasons. RST=1 means the connection should be reset.

- *PSH* Push Function. PSH=1 tells a receiving TCP to immediately deliver the data of this segment to the receiving ULP. It may be used to indicate that no additional data will come from the sending ULP immediately.

- *FIN* Used to terminate connections. FIN=1 means that the Sender will not transmit any more ULP data.

Window   Abbrev: WNDW

Field size = 16 bits
  Units = Octets
  Range = 0 - 2**16-1

- This value represents the number of data octets, beginning with the one indicated in the Acknowledgment field, which the Sender is willing to accept.

- Window is the *flow control* parameter of TCP.

- Window is a relatively lengthy field because it counts the number of bytes that may be received beyond the currently acknowledged byte, rather than merely counting the number of packets that may still be sent, as is done by XNS' SPP.

Checksum

Field size = 16 bits

- A *checksum* field is applied to all 16 bit words in the header and data. The checksum also covers a 96 bit pseudo header conceptually prefixed to the TCP header. This pseudo header contains the Source Address, Destination Address, Protocol ID and the TCP segment length.

- *Checksum* contains the 16-bit one's complement of the one's complement sum of all 16-bit words in the header and text.

Urgent Pointer   Abbrev: URGPTR

> *Field size* = 16 bits
> *Units* = Octets
> *Range* = 0 - 2**16-1

- This field specifies the last byte of urgent data.

- The value of the *Urgent Pointer* is a positive offset from the *Sequence Number* in this segment. Adding the pointer value to the sequence number yields the sequence number of the last urgent data octet. This field is only to be interpreted in segments with the URG Control flag set.

Options   Abbrev: OPT

> *Field size* = variable

- If present, *Options* occupy space at the end of the TCP header. All Options are included in the checksum. An Option may begin on any octet boundary.

- The *Options* field is reserved for miscellaneous things. The only interesting official option currently defined communicates the Maximum Segment Size and is sent during connection establishment.

Connection Management

TCP's main function is to provide data connections (communication channels) between pairs of ULPs. Connection management can be broken into three phases: *Connection Establishment, Connection Maintenance* and *Connection Termination.*

Connections are endowed with certain properties that apply for the lifetime of the connection, including security and precedence levels. These properties are specified by the ULPs at connection opening. TCP provides a means for a ULP to actively initiate a connection to another ULP uniquely named with a socket. A socket is actually the concatenation of an IP address (found in the IP Header) with the application's port number (from the TCP Header). A connection is defined by the combination of the two participants' socket numbers.

TCP actively establishes a connection to the named ULP if:

- no connection between the two named sockets already exits;

- internal TCP resources are sufficient; and

- the other ULP has simultaneously executed a matching active open to the ULP, or previously executed a global unspecified (or matching, passive) open. (An active open is sometimes termed a *call* in other transport terminologies; a passive open is termed a *listen.*)

TCP provides a means for a ULP to listen passively for, and respond to, active connection attempts from correspondent ULPs. A ULP may be interested in calls from a particular remote correspondent, or from just any remote correspondent. It thus has two types of passive opens which it can perform.

1. *Fully specified* — a calling ULP is uniquely identified by a socket. A connection will be accepted only when an active open is received (as described above) from the specific remote socket.

2. *Unspecified* — no socket is specified. A connection is established with any remote ULP executing a matching active open identifying this ULP.

Once a connection has been established, TCP will maintain it as long as both parties are interested in keeping it active. Connections which are established but which are not actively sending user data do not generate any packets. This is not a problem, but it is interesting that TCP does not specify a mechanism for detecting the loss of a connection partner when no data are being exchanged. But since for some applications such information is of use, some TCP implementations use a trick to accomplish this detection. They send a datagram with no data and an incorrect sequence number. TCP specifies that the recipient must respond with a datagram indicating the correct sequence number. If no response is received, the probing TCP may be able to decide that its peer has disappeared.

Established connections can be terminated in either of two ways:

1. *Graceful Close* — Both ULPs close their side of the duplex connection, either simultaneously or sequentially, when data transfer is complete. TCP coordinates connection termination and prevents loss of data in transit.

2. *Abort* — When one ULP unilaterally forces closure of the connection, TCP does not coordinate connection termination. Data in transit may be lost.

TCP builds its services on top of the Network Layer's potentially unreliable services with mechanisms such as error detection, positive acknowledgements, sequence numbers and flow control. These mechanisms require addressing and control information to be initialized and maintained during data transfer, as described in the following paragraphs which also describe the operation of the major TCP mechanisms and services.

Acknowledgement

TCP employs a *Positive Acknowledgement with Retransmission* (PAR) mechanism to recover from the loss of data by the lower layers. PAR allows a sending host's TCP to retransmit data at timed intervals until a positive acknowledgment is returned. In order to avoid unnecessary retransmissions and excessive retransmission delays, TCP dynamically adjusts the timeout to estimate the segment round-trip time plus a factor for internal processing. A simple checksum detects segments damaged in transit and discards them without acknowledgment. PAR, therefore, treats damaged segments the same as lost segments and compensates for their loss.

The great variety of networks supported by TCP — for example, Ethernet, Satellite nets, Land-based long-haul nets — differ greatly with respect to throughput, delay, etc. The delay for Ethernet will be in milliseconds, for example, which differs greatly from remote connections through multiple satellite links, which can amount to several seconds when the Internet is congested. TCP specifies adaptive techniques for delays so one does not send and resend too quickly, or too slowly. TCP specifies an adaptive retransmission algorithm which includes exponential backoff, which is similar to the exponential backoff in Ethernet.

The sequence numbers used by TCP extend the PAR mechanism by allowing a single acknowledgment to cover all previously received data. Thus, a sending TCP can send new data even when previous data have not been specifically acknowledged. An acknowledgment refers to all previous data, rather than to a recent segment of data. Therefore, receivers can refrain from sending a large number of acknowledgements.

Flow Control

TCP's flow control mechanism permits a receiving TCP to govern the amount of data dispatched by a sending TCP. The mechanism is based on a window which defines a contiguous range of acceptable sequence numbered data. As data are accepted, TCP slides the window upward in the sequence number space. The current window is specified in every segment and enables peer TCPs to maintain up-to-date information. There is a recommended mechanism for preventing the Silly Window Syndrome which can otherwise greatly increase segment-handling overhead as window allotments grow and shrink. This syndrome results from overly-quick sending of window modifications and can cause the sender to issue many small datagrams rather than a few large ones.

Multiplexing

TCP's multiplexing mechanism provides for multiple ULPs and processes within a single host. It also permits multiple processes in a ULP to use TCP simultaneously. The mechanism relates identifiers, called ports, to ULP's processes accessing TCP services. A ULP connection is uniquely identified with a socket — the concatenation of a port number and an IP address. Each connection is uniquely named with a socket pair — that is, the source and destination sockets.

This identifying scheme allows a single ULP to support connections to multiple remote ULPs. It also permits two processes to have multiple connections with each other. ULPs which receive connections for popular resources are assigned permanent Well-Known Ports.

Synchronization

Two ULPs who wish to communicate instruct their respective TCPs to initialize and synchronize the connection information required to obtain an established virtual circuit. Since the potentially unreliable network layer may attempt to deliver old data from previous connections, the TCP connection is opened using a handshake procedure with clock-based sequence numbers. This reduces the possibility that delayed packet arrivals will appear to be valid packets within the current connection.

In the simplest handshake, the TCP pair synchronizes sequence numbers by exchanging three segments. The procedure, therefore, is called the three-way handshake. The three-way handshake works on the basis of the fact that both machines when attempting to open a communication channel transmit *Sequence Numbers* (SEQ) and *Acknowledge Numbers* (ACK), as illustrated and explained in Figure 4-6.

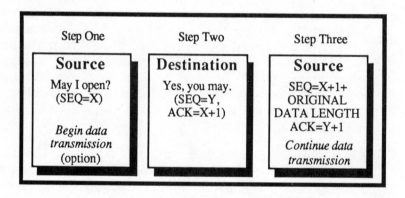

Figure 4-6. Three-way Handshake

Rendezvous

A ULP can open a connection in one of two modes, *passive* or *active*. With an active open, a ULP instructs its TCP to actively initiate a three-way handshake to connect to another ULP. A passive open instructs the TCP to await a connection attempt initiated by an active caller. The active/passive feature is useful for server-oriented applications. A remote database management program, for example, might passively await active connection attempts by database users at remote workstations. The three-way handshake also coordinates two simultaneous active opens between peer TCPs.

The Push Flag

Use of the Push Flag is another part of the segmentation function. TCP normally groups data transparently into segments for transmission at its own convenience. However, with a *push* a ULP can expedite delivery by forcing TCP to package and send data handed it up to that point without waiting any longer for further data. For example, a terminal serving ULP may want to *push* characters a line-at-a-time to a remote application serving ULP.

Two mechanisms are required. First the source ULP must have an implementation specific mechanism for telling its local TCP to send the data, and then the sending TCP must be able to tell the receiving TCP to deliver the data. The Push Flag is used for the second purpose.

User Datagram Protocol (UDP)

UDP provides low overhead transaction service to allow ULPs to send datagrams between one another. Like TCP, UDP employs port fields for specifying the source and destination processes of each transaction. An optional checksum is also employed.

The Transport Level

Port Numbers

TCP and UDP both have Port Numbers, to distinguish among different data exchange participants. Since IP Protocol ID is evaluated before Port Number, the TCP and UDP uses of the 16-bit values are independent. That is, the same Port Number can involve two different processes, if one uses the number for TCP and the other uses it for UDP.

Furthermore, the selection of Port Numbers is restricted. The values 0-255 are reserved for assignment by the Department of Defense; they are called *Well-Known Ports*. A subset is listed in *Appendix Two*. Any program which uses a Well-Known Port must conform to the specified, higher-level protocol. Note that there is an attempt to coordinate the assignment of Well-Known Ports between TCP and UDP.

Many operating systems include the Well-Known Ports among a set of protected ports. These may be accessed only by processes which have special operating system privileges. The remaining Port Numbers, called *Ephemeral Port Numbers*, may be used by any process.

Levels Five through Seven — Session through Application Layers

Session, *Presentation* and *Application* Layers are found at levels five through seven of the ISO Reference Model (see Figure 5-1).

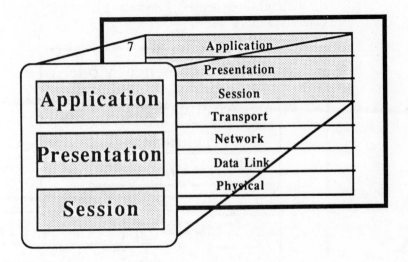

Figure 5-1. The Top Layers

Services Identified with the Session, Presentation and Application Levels

Network services offered at the lower levels are fairly dis-crete. In the case of the top three Layers of the ISO Refer-ence Model, however, services sometimes do not keep within level boundaries very well. These higher levels have very few standard specifications and so TCP/IP ser-vices offered at these levels necessarily transcend the divid-ing line between the levels. NetBios, for example, has to do with all three levels. Figure 5-2 illustrates the services offered at this level.

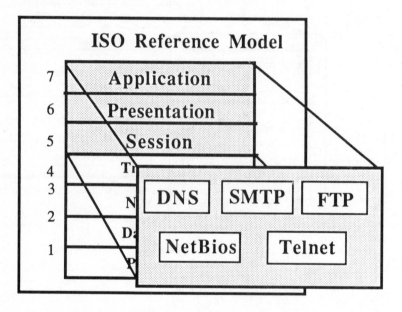

Figure 5-2. Upper Layer Services

The *Session Layer*, at Level Five, is concerned with dialogue management and resource location. The Session Layer enables programs to establish connections with one another by the use of names instead of socket addresses, and to manage their interaction with one another using such concepts as *checkpoint* and *restart*. The Session Layer within TCP/IP has no standardized protocols for these kinds of functions, though interim resource location (name lookup) protocols are becoming widely implemented. A connection between two Presentation Layer processes is called a Session. The Session Layer is responsible for maintaining, as well as establishing and disestablishing, the Session.

The *Presentation Layer*, level six, identifies functions that a user might frequently need to perform, such as transformation services — including, for example, text compression, conversion between character codes (e.g. ASCII to EBCDIC) and device conversion (changing such things as line and screen length, end of line convention, scroll versus page mode, character sets and cursor addressing).

The *Application Layer* is where the core of the application programs the computer is running reside. Standards and rigid specifications can hardly be imposed upon this layer although individual standards are defined here. For example, in order to operate a relational database distributed among a number of machines, it is necessary to specify the appropriate protocols and consider that they logically reside at the Application Layer.

The real work of the TCP hosts gets done at the higher levels of the protocol stack. The FTP, Telnet, SMTP and DNS Protocols in particular are widely enough implemented that the interworking of multi-vendor equipment is done better with TCP/IP than by any other current protocol suite. Many other protocols are defined within the TCP/IP suite. This section describes only the most popular. The Assigned Port Numbers listed in Appendix Two refer to several other important protocols. For a complete list see RFC 991, *Official ARPA-Internet Protocols*.

File Transfer Protocol (FTP)

The *File Transfer Protocol* (FTP — Mil-Std #1780) controls the exchange of files between two hosts. It does not assume a set system configuration. FTP employs two TCP connections to get its work done — one for exchanging commands and responses and the other for moving files. FTP provides a number of important services, including the following:

FTP Control Connections

FTP employs a User/Server model, which thus contains *User FTP* and *Server FTP* components. The User FTP activates the transfer process and the Server FTP responds. User FTPs typically supply an interactive interface to users so the users can demand the transfer of files to or from the remote host.

When a User FTP is instructed to begin file transfers with a particular remote host, it opens a *control* connection to the Server FTP listening at a Well-Known Port on the remote host. It exchanges commands and responses with the Server FTP on this connection for purposes of identifying its user, providing file names and specifying the nature of the desired file system operation (*store, retrieve, append, delete,* etc.).

FTP Data Connections

When a transfer is to be performed, the User and Server FTPs establish a second TCP connection to support it. They use the control connection to specify the port numbers for this data connection and to describe the file transfer parameters (*binary, ASCII,* etc.).

The User FTP, or its designate, listens on the specified data port; the Server initiates the data connection and transfer in accordance with the specified parameters. It

Levels Five through Seven

should be noted that the data port need not be in the same host as the User FTP, though the user or the User FTP process must ensure that there is an appropriate listen outstanding at the specified data port. It should also be noted that the data connection may be used for simultaneous sending and receiving.

Note how users might wish to transfer files between two hosts, neither of which is their local host. They can accomplish this by setting up command connections to the two servers and then arranging for a data connection between them.

Telnet

The purpose of the Telnet Protocol Standard is to provide a fairly general, bidirectional, eight-bit byte-oriented communications facility. The protocol provides a standard method of interfacing among terminal devices and terminal-oriented processes. It also supports linking (terminal-to-terminal) and distributed computation (process-to-process) communication.

A Telnet connection is a TCP connection used to transmit data with interspersed Telnet control information. The Telnet Protocol is built upon three main ideas: the concept of a *Network Virtual Terminal*; the principle of *negotiated options*; and a *symmetrical view* of terminals and processes.

Network Virtual Terminal (NVT)

In most cases, Telnet is used to connect terminals to hosts. When a Telnet connection is first established, each end is assumed to originate and terminate at a Network Virtual Terminal (NVT). An NVT is an imaginary device which provides a standard, network-wide, intermediate representation of a canonical terminal. This eliminates the need for Server and User hosts to keep information about the characteristics of each other's terminals and terminal handling conventions. All hosts, both User and Server, map their local device characteristics and conventions so as to appear to be dealing with an NVT over the network, and each can assume a similar mapping by the other. The NVT strikes a balance between being overly restrictive (not providing hosts a rich enough vocabulary for mapping into their local character sets) and being overly inclusive (penalizing users with modest terminals).

When Telnet is used to connect a terminal to a computer, a *User Telnet* program translates the characters used by the terminal into the character set of the NVT, and delivers the NVT characters to its remote peer (over the TCP connection). This peer, the Server Telnet program, must translate the NVT characters into ones used by its host, and deliver the characters into the host's operating system as though they had been generated by a locally attached device.

Principle of Negotiated Options

Telnet allows hosts to select services over and above those available within an NVT and, for users with sophisticated terminals, to select elegant over minimal services. Various sanctioned options are independent of, but structured within, the Telnet Protocol. Telnet employs a *do/don't, will/ won't* negotiation permitting a client and server to agree to use different sets of conventions for a Telnet connection. That is, the sender says that it will or won't perform some option, or it instructs the other host to do an option, or not. This elegant mechanism permits the recipient of the option request to respond (in the negative) without having to understand anything about the requested option.

Such options might include changing the character set, the echo mode, the line length, etc. The basic strategy for setting up the use of options is to have either or both parties initiate a request that some option take effect. The other party may then either accept or reject the request. If the request is accepted, the option immediately takes effect; if it is rejected, the associated aspect of the connection remains as specified for an NVT. Clearly, a party may always refuse a request to enable and must never refuse a request to disable some option since all parties must be prepared to support the NVT.

The syntax of option negotiation ensures that if both parties simultaneously request an option, each will see the other's request as the positive acknowledgment of its own.

While many options have been defined, the minimum recommended set permits binary (transparent) transmission, remote character echoing, disabling of a logical half-duplex line turn around, acquisition of status, and transmission of a timing mark. An example of the potential complexity of an option is the increasing use of one that permits emulation of IBM 3270-type terminals.

NetBios

DOS, the *Disk Operating System* provided by Microsoft for IBM and compatible PCs, has recently been extended to include a set of system calls which allow application programs to gain access to networking services. The set of system calls is collectively referred to as *NetBios*. NetBios provides the means for applications on different PCs to efficiently and effectively seek out and talk to one another as peers.

Like the ISO Reference Model, NetBios provides a service specification (ostensibly at the Session Level upper interface) without specifying the use of any particular underlying protocols. This means that the services can be implemented on top of any number of different networking technologies. *Ungermann-Bass*, for example, provides NetBios implementations on all three IEEE local area networking technologies (including Ethernet) and over all three popular protocol stacks (*XNS*, *TCP/IP* and *ISO*).

Some of the Session Level services offered by NetBios have no counterpart in the current set of protocols standardized within the TCP/IP family. For example, NetBios implementations must be able to tell a called application the string name of the calling application. To provide these services, it has been necessary to invent new protocols beyond those in the standard suite.

To maintain multi-vendor interoperability, it is desirable to standardize on these extensions. RFCs 1001 and 1002 offer a proposal for how these extensions should be done so that hosts can also have NetBios types of services and can then supply applications which serve as peers to those actually running on PCs.

Among the many extensions being standardized are ones which suggest that resource location be provided by consultation with a *Name Server*. NetBios implementations need to register the names of their applications with such a server, and need to interrogate the server to learn the IP Address (and port) of named applications which they want to call. A number of commercial implementations of Name Servers which support NetBios names are available and are typically packaged with a PC, as was depicted earlier in Figure 1-6, p. 12.

Also depicted in that figure was the notion of a PC File Server. Microsoft's own File Redirector is one of the most important PC programs that calls on NetBios for its networking services. This operating system extension allows DOS to place its files on a remote PC (the server) and to access the files on behalf of PC applications, just as though they were located locally. The combination of this file redirection with the ability for host-based TCP modules to participate in the NetBios standards has resulted in new products wherein hosts can serve as file repositories for PCs.

Domain Name Service (DNS)

The DNS, which is an example of a naming protocol, provides Name-to-IP-Address translation. Importantly, DNS also permits decentralized administration of resource names and specifies redundancy of Servers as a way of providing a reliable query service for users. The initial purpose of the DNS is to permit mail-sending hosts to discover the IP Addresses of mail-receiving and mail-forwarding hosts. It is mentioned here because of its recognized growing potential to serve many other purposes, even ones involving NetBios names.

Decentralization of name administration is accomplished by use of multiple name fields, with each field further specifying a sub-domain. The 'top-level' domain is centrally administered by the DDN *Network Information Center* (NIC) which assigns administrative responsibility for immediately-subordinate sub-domains. Administrators for these sub-domains may, in turn, create further partitioning through additional sub-domains. For example, the domain 'COM' is a top-level domain which encompasses commercial members and 'UB.COM' is the NIC-assigned name which refers to Ungermann-Bass. Ungermann-Bass may, in turn, assign subordinate names. Thus, 'Engr.UB. COM' might refer to machines that are used by Engineering and 'Mktg. UB.COM.' might refer to those used by Marketing.

Simple Mail Transport
Protocol (SMTP)

The Internet standard for electronic mail is a simple, text-oriented protocol designed to transfer mail reliably and efficiently. As an Application Layer service, SMTP does not care what particular Transport service is underneath it. It can be used over a TCP connection to transmit mail across a network, or just as easily used over any interprocess communication channel to transfer mail between processes within a single machine.

Levels Five through Seven

Each piece of mail is sent after some negotiation about who the original sender is, and who the recipients should be. When an SMTP server process agrees to accept mail for a particular recipient, it assumes responsibility for posting the mail to the user if the user is local, or forwarding the mail if the user is not local. As a message travels over a network, a reverse path is carried along so it is possible to notify the original sender of any failure.

Each mail message typically has a *header* and a *body*. The header contains information found typically on memos — *TO, FROM, CC* and *SUBJECT*. RFC # 822, *Specification of the Formation for Internet Text Messages*, specifies the syntax for header fields. The *body* is free-form and may contain ASCII text.

Appendix One — Glossary of Terms

Acknowledgement Number

A value carried in the TCP Header that identifies for a TCP Sender the sequence number of the byte which the TCP Receiver expects next.

Acknowledgement Flag (ACK)

A bit in the Control Flags field of the TCP Header indicating that the accompanying Acknowledgement Number Field contains an Acknowledgement Number.

Baseband

A digital signalling technique used in Ethernet LANs.

Broadband

An analog signalling technique used in IEEE Token Bus LANs. Analog techniques allow a single medium to be used for several information signals at once just as, for example, in cable TV systems.

Broadcast

A name for a Data Link Layer frame which is addressed to all stations attached to that Data Link.

Bus

A linear topology for a local area network wiring scheme.

Channel

A path for electrical transmission. Baseband systems provide a single channel on a physical medium. Broadband systems provide multiple channels (by use of frequency division) on a physical medium.

Checksum

A bit pattern which is computed according to the contents of a packet and which serves to help the packet's receiver detect whether the contents of the packet are as originally sent.

Connection

A logical communication path between two hosts provided by TCP modules in each.

CSMA/CD

Carrier Sense Multiple Access with Collision Detection. The technique used by Ethernet stations to control access to their shared communication channel. They listen before transmitting (and refrain from using the channel if it's already in use), and listen during transmission (to determine whether their own signal is being corrupted by somebody else's). If such a *collision* is detected, the station will stop its transmission and attempt it again sometime later.

Datagram

A unit of information sent from one IP module to another.

Data Offset

A field of the TCP Header which reveals the distance (expressed in units of 32-bits) from the start of a TCP Header to the end of the Header (and thus the beginning of the accompanying data).

Destination Address

The IP header field containing an internet address indicating where a datagram is to be sent.

Destination Port

The TCP or UDP header field containing a two-octet value identifying the destination upper level service or program.

Don't Fragment Flag (DF)

A bit in the Control Flags field of the TCP Header that indicates to IP modules whether or not a datagram can be fragmented.

Ethernet

A baseband, CSMA/CD local area network which allows up to 1,024 stations to send frames to one another with digital signalling rates of 10 million bits per second.

Finished Flag (FIN)

A bit in the Control Flags field of the TCP Header that indicates that the TCP Sender is done transmitting on the TCP connection. The connection is considered terminated when a FIN has been sent in each direction.

Fragment

An IP datagram which contains a part of the data sent by a Transport module as a discrete request. IP produces fragments when the Transport request is too large to be held in a single datagram.

Fragmentation

The process of breaking a datagram into smaller pieces and attaching new Internet Headers to form smaller datagrams. Fragmentation permits the transfer of a datagram over a subnetwork that has a maximum packet size too small for the complete datagram. IP requires that receivers be able to reassemble datagrams.

Fragmentation Offset

A field in the IP Header marking the relative position of a datagram fragment within the larger original datagram.

FTP

The *File Transfer Protocol*. User and Server FTP programs use this protocol on top of TCP to send files to one another.

FTP Commands

A set of commands and responses which flow between a User-FTP and a Server-FTP on their Control Connection.

Gateway

A device, or pair of devices, which interconnect two or more networks or subnetworks enabling the passage of data from one (sub)network to another. A gateway contains an IP module, a routing protocol module and (for each connected subnetwork) a *Subnetwork Protocol* module (SNP). The routing protocol is used to coordinate with other gateways. A gateway is often called an IP Router.

Header

The collection of control information transmitted, with data, between peer entities.

Host

A computer, particularly a source or destination of messages on a communications network.

ICMP

The *Internet Control Message Protocol*. The collection of messages exchanged by IP modules in both hosts and gateways in order to report errors, problems and operating information.

Internet Header Length (IHL)

The value contained in the IP Header that tells the length of the Header in 32-bit words.

Internetwork

A set of interconnected, logically independent, networks. The constituent networks are usually administrated separately and may be composed of different transmission media.

Internet Address

A four-octet (32-bit) source or destination address composed of a Network field and a host field. The latter may be further divided to include a local subnetwork address.

IP

Internet Protocol — The standard used for sending the basic unit of data, an IP datagram, through an internet.

ISN

The Initial Sequence Number. The first sequence number used for either sending or receiving on a TCP connection.

ISO Reference Model (also, *OSI Reference Model*)

The *International Standards Organization Reference Model for Open Systems Interconnection* — A standard approach to network design which introduces modularity by dividing the complex set of functions into more manageable, self-contained, functional layers, as follows:

1. *Physical* **Layer** — the level at which protocols provide the mechanical and electrical means by which devices are physically connected and data is transmitted.

2. *Data Link* **Layer** — the level at which information is moved reliably across the physical link.

3. *Network* **Layer** — the level at which connections between systems are established, maintained and terminated; concerned with switching and routing information.

4. *Transport* **Layer** — the level at which end-to-end data integrity and quality of service are ensured.

5. *Session* **Layer** — the level which standardizes the tasks of setting up a session and terminating it; coordinates interaction between end-application processes.

6. *Presentation* **Layer** — the level at which the character set and data code are specified — as well as the way data is displayed on a screen or printer.

7. *Application* **layer** — concerned with the higher level functions which provide support to the application of system activities.

LAN

Local Area Network; A network connecting various electronic devices in a localized geographical area such as a single office building or a campus.

Long Haul Network

A network which usually spans large geographic distances and involves low speed store and forward transmission mechanisms.

Maximum Segment Lifetime (MSL)

The maximum amount of time an IP datagram may exist within an Internet. The default *MSL* is set at two minutes.

Maximum Segment Size (MSS)

The maximum size of the TCP segments to be exchanged by TCP peers. TCP modules who want to accommodate system concerns for buffering or subnet constraints on maximum datagram size may negotiate the default of 65,536 to a smaller value.

Maximum Transmission Unit (MTU)

A subnetwork dependent value which indicates the largest datagram that a subnetwork can handle.

More Fragments Flag (MF)

A bit in the Control Flags field of the TCP Header which indicates whether or not a datagram fragment contains the final portion of data from its original unfragmented datagram.

Network Virtual Terminal

The *Network Virtual Terminal* as defined in the Telnet Protocol (Mil-Std 1782). NVT specifies a standard form for ASCII representation and for certain other characteristics of a simple, canonical terminal.

Options

The optional set of fields at the end of the IP Header used to carry control or routing data or, at the end of the TCP Header, used in a SYN segment to carry the maximum segment size acceptable to the sender. An Options field in IP may contain none, one, or several options, and each option may be one to several octets in length. The options allow ULPs to customize the services of TCP or IP. The options are also useful in testing situations to carry diagnostic data such as timestamping.

OSI Reference Model

Cf. ISO Reference Model.

Point-to-point

Transmission of data between a single Sender and Receiver. A Point-to-point Link is a circuit connecting only two stations to each other with no intermediary node.

Port

The identifier used to select a particular process within a TCP/IP host.

Public Data Network (PDN)

An X.25-based, long haul packet switching network.

Push Flag (PSH)

A bit in the Control Flags of the TCP Header which indicates that the accompanying data should be quickly passed by a receiving TCP to its client ULP.

Reassembly

The process of piecing together datagram fragments to reproduce the original large datagram. Reassembly is guided by fragmentation parameters carried in the datagram's IP Headers.

Reliability

One service quality parameter provided by the Type of Service mechanism in IP. The reliability parameter can be set to one of four levels: lowest, low, high or highest. It appears as a two-bit field within the Type of Service field in the IP Header.

Ring

A circular or positional topology for a local area network wiring scheme.

Reset FLAG (RST)

A bit in the Control Flags of the TCP Header which indicates that the connection associated with this segment is to be terminated and any unacknowledged data discarded.

Segment

The unit of data exchanged by TCP modules. The term may also be used to describe the unit of exchange between any transport protocol modules. A TCP segment maps into one IP datagram.

Sequence Number

A value carried in the TCP Header that identifies for a TCP Receiver the position in the ULP byte stream of the first byte contained in the received TCP segment.

Server-FTP Process

A process or set of processes which perform the function of file transfer in cooperation with a user-FTP process and, possibly, another Server.

Socket

The concatenation of IP Address and TCP port which together specify a particular process or service within the Internet.

Stream Delivery Service

The special handling required for a class of volatile periodic traffic typified by voice. The class requires the maximum acceptable delay to be only slightly larger than the minimum propagation time, or requires a small allowable variance in packet interarrival time.

Station

A network node.

TCP

Transmission Control Protocol. A transport protocol providing connection-oriented, end-to-end reliable byte data transmission in packet-switched computer subnetworks and internetworks.

Telnet

An Upper Layer Protocol used typically by terminal servers and hosts to provide interactive access by terminal users to host application programs.

Token Bus

A local area network in which permission to transmit is specifically passed from one station to another as a means for governing shared access to the channel.

Token Ring

A local area network in which permission to transmit is implicitly passed among the stations by virtue of their positional relationship to one another.

Topology

A description of how stations on a network connect to a cable. Examples of specific topologies include: *Bus*, *Ring*, *Star* and *Tree*. Two kinds of topology include:

1. *Physical topology* — The configuration of network nodes and links. Description of the physical geometric arrangement of the links and nodes that make up a network, as determined by their physical connections.

2. *Logical topology* — Description of the possible connections between network nodes, indicating which pairs of nodes are able to communicate, whether or not they have a direct physical connection.

Total Length

An IP Header field containing the number of octets in an internet datagram, including both the IP Header and the Data portion.

Type of Service

An IP Header field containing the transmission quality parameters, precedence level, reliability level, speed level, resource tradeoff (precedence vs. reliability) and transmission mode (datagram vs. stream).

Upper Layer Protocol (ULP)

Any protocol above IP or TCP in the Layered Protocol Hierarchy that uses IP or TCP. This term includes Transport Layer protocols, Session Layer protocols, Presentation Layer protocols and Application Layer protocol.

Urgent Pointer

A TCP Header field containing a positive offset to the sequence number of the last urgent data octet in the connection's data stream, relative to the sequence number of the current segment. This field is valid only when the URG flag is on.

Urgent Flag (URG)

A bit in the Control Field of the TCP Header which indicates that the TCP Header contains an Urgent Pointer.

User Datagram Protocol (UDP)

A transaction-based Transport Level Protocol within the TCP/IP Protocol Suite.

User-FTP Process

A set of functions including a protocol interpreter, a data transfer process and a user interface which together perform the function of file transfer in cooperation with one or more Server FTP processes. The user interface allows a local language to be used in command-reply dialogue with the user.

Virtual Circuit

A network service enabling two end points to communicate as though via a physical circuit; a logical transmission path.

Window

A two-octet field of the TCP Header indicating the number of data octets (relative to the acknowledgment number in the Header) that the segment sender is currently willing to accept.

X.25

A CCITT standard which defines the interface between a Public Data Network and a packet-mode user device. Defines the services that these user devices can expect from the Public Data Network, including the ability to establish virtual circuits, to move data from one device to another and to destroy the virtual circuit when through.

Appendix Two —
Assigned Numbers

Many protocols have fields of information that specify categorical information. Different values in the field indicate different categories of related activity. For example, within a layered protocol suite, a protocol at one level usually needs a field that specifies the next-higher level protocol.

Such fields usually have a subset of their values reserved for assignment by an official office or standards body. For TCP/IP, an RFC, called 'Assigned Numbers' indicates the official values that are relevant to the DoD Internet Protocol Suite. At the time this paper was written, RFC 990, November 1986 was the latest version of the RFC.

A few of these assigned numbers are included in this Appendix for convenient reference.

Ethernet Type Numbers
of Interest

Hex Value	Description
0600	XEROX Network Systems, Internet Datagram Protocol
0800	DoD IP
0806	ARP
8035	RARP (Reverse ARP)

Assigned Protocol Numbers Within the IP Header

Decimal Keyword Description

Decimal	Keyword	Description
0		Reserved
1	*ICMP*	Internet Control Message
5	*ST*	Stream
6	*TCP*	Transmission Control Protocol
8	*EGP*	Exterior Gateway Protocol
9	*IGP*	Any private interior gateway protocol
11	*NVP*	Network Voice Protocol
17	*UDP*	User Datagram Protocol
20	*HMP*	Host Monitoring Protocol
22	*XNS-IDP*	Xerox Network Systems Internet Datagram Protocol
27	*RDP*	Reliable Data Protocol
28	*IRTP*	Internet Reliable Transaction Protocol
29	*ISO-TP4*	ISO Transport Protocol Class 4
30	*NETBLT*	Bulk Data Transfer Protocol
61		Any host internal protocol

Assigned Numbers

Assigned Port Numbers in TCP and UDP Headers

Decimal	Keyword	Description
7	*Echo*	Echo
9	*Discard*	Discard
13	*Daytime*	Daytime
15	*Netstat*	Who is up?
17	*Quote*	Quote of the Day
20	*FTP-Data*	File Transfer (Default Data)
21	*FTP*	File Transfer (Control)
23	*Telnet*	Telnet
25	*SMTP*	Simple Mail Transfer Protocol
37	*Time*	Time of Day
39	*RLP*	Resource Location Protocol
42	*Nameserver*	Host Name Server
46	*MPM-Snd*	MPM (default send)
53	*Domain*	Domain Name Server
67	*BootPS*	Bootstrap Protocol Server
68	*BootPC*	Bootstrap Protocol Client
69	*TFTP*	Trivial File Transfer
79	*Finger*	Who is on System
101	*Hostname*	NIC Host Name Server
102	*ISO-TSAP*	ISO-TSAP
103	*X400*	X400
104	*X400-SND*	X400-SND
105	*CSNET-NS*	CSNet Name Server
109	*POP-2*	Post Office Protocol, Version 2
113	*AUTH*	Authentication Service
115	*SFTP*	Simple File Transfer Protocol
119	*NNTGP*	Network News Trans. Protocol
123	*NTP*	Network Time Protocol
129	*PWDGEN*	Password Generator protocol

Assigned Telnet Options

Options	Names
0	Binary Transmission
1	Echo
2	Reconnection
3	Suppress Go Ahead
4	Approx Message Size Negotiation
5	Status
6	Timing Mark
7	Remote Controlled Transmission and Echo
8	Output Line Width
9	Output Page Size
10	Output Carriage-Return Disposition
11	Output Horizontal Tab Stops
12	Output Horizontal Tab Disposition
13	Output Formfeed disposition
14	Output Vertical Tabstops
15	Output Vertical Tab Disposition
16	Output Linefeed Disposition
17	Extended ASCII
18	Logout
19	Byte Macro
20	Data Entry Terminal
24	Terminal Type
25	End of Record
27	Output Marking
28	Terminal Location Number
255	Extended-Options-List

Assigned Numbers

Appendix Three — References

Most of the technical information necessary to understand and implement the TCP/IP protocol suites is specified in

DDN Protocol Handbook, Vol. 1-3, December, 1985

Copies may be ordered from:

DDN Network Information Center
SRI International, Room EJ291
333 Ravenswood Avenue
Menlo Park, CA 94025
Telephone: (800) 235-3155

Price, $110.00. Make checks payable to *SRI International.*

This paper has referred to a few Requests for Comments which are not part of the *DDN Protocol Handbook.* The NIC provides services for obtaining these, and other, RFCs. A subscription service is available.

RFC 893 *Trailer Encapsulation*; S.J. Leffler & M.J. Karels, April 1984.

RFC 950 *Internet Standard Subnetting Procedure*; J. Mogul & J. Postel, August 1985.

RFC 990 *Assigned Numbers*; J. Reynolds & J. Postel, November 1986.

RFC 991 *Official ARPA-Internet Protocols*; J. Reynolds & J. Postel, November, 1986.

RFC 1001 *Protocol Standard for a NetBios Service on a TCP/UDP Transport: Concepts and Methods*; March 1987.

RFC 1002 *Protocol Standard for a NetBios Service on a TCP/UDP Transport: Detailed Specifications;* March 1987.

IEN 116 *Internet Name Server;* J. Postel, August 1979.

Early papers about TCP/IP include:

Cerf, V. and R. Kahn, "A Protocol for Pocket Network Intercommunication," *IEEE Transactions on Communication,* May 1974.

Davidson, J., Hathaway, W, Postel, J., Minmo, N., Thomas, R. and Walden, D., "The ARPANET Telnet Protocol: Its Purpose, Principles, Implementation and Impact on Host Operating System Design," *Proceedings of 5th Data Communications Symposium,* Snowbird, UT, Sept. 1977.

Leiner, B., J. Postel, R. Cole and O. Mills, "The DARPA Internet Protocol Suite," *Proceedings of INFOCOM 85.* IEEE, Washington, D.C., March 1985.

Postel, J., C. Sunshine and O. Cohen, "The ARPA Internet Protocol," *Computer Networks,* Vol. 5, No. 4, July 1981.

Index